NUTCRACKER
Activity Book

Victoria Fremont
and
Cathy Beylon

DOVER PUBLICATIONS, INC.
Mineola, New York

Bibliographical Note

Nutcracker Activity Book is a new work, first published by Dover
Publications, Inc., in 1999.

International Standard Book Number: 0-486-40494-3

Manufactured in the United States of America
Dover Publications, Inc., 31 East 2nd Street, Mineola, N.Y. 11501

NOTE

Let this little activity book bring to life the story of the Nutcracker Ballet, long a family favorite during the Christmas season. Young fans can thrill to the battle between the Nutcracker and the Mouse King, and can savor a visit with Clara and the Prince to the Kingdom of Sweets. The puzzles in this book offer challenge and fun. If you need help, or if you want to check your answers, the solutions begin on page 55.

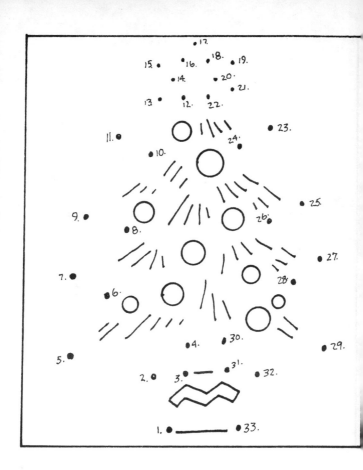

Connect the dots to see what Clara and Fritz
found in their living room on Christmas eve.

Only two of these nutcrackers are exactly
alike. Find and circle them.

5

Help the Nutcracker find his way through the
maze to capture the Mouse King.

Can you find 5 ballet slippers hidden among
the party guests?

7

There are 3 things wrong at Clara's
and Fritz's Christmas dinner. Can you find
and circle them?

Here's the many-headed Mouse King.
Count his heads and write the number
on the line._____

1. CLOWN

2. WAGON

3. PONY

4. DRUM

5. YO-YO

Clara and Fritz received many Christmas gifts. Look at the pictures above and fill in

1. ___ L O W N
2. W ___ G O N
3. P O ___ Y
4. ___ R U M
5. ___ O - Y O

the puzzle. The letters in the boxes will tell
you what's in their stockings.

11

Fritz is asleep. Can you find 3 candy canes
and 3 lollipops hidden in his room?

12

Help Clara and the Prince find their way
to the Kingdom of Sweets.

Look carefully at the 2 pictures
of the Stahlbaum family's Christmas tree.

14

Find 6 ways in which they are different.

15

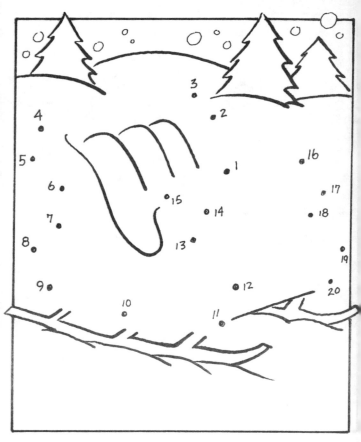

Fritz received a special gift to play with in the snow. Connect the dots to see what it is.

Among Clara's dolls, 2 are exactly alike.
Find and circle them.

17

A great battle is being fought between
the toy soldiers and the mice!

18

How many soldiers do you count?_____
How many mice do you count?_____
How many are there all together?_____ 19

NUTCRACKER

CAKE

_____ _____
_____ _____
_____ _____
_____ _____

How many words can you spell using
the letters in the word NUTCRACKER?
One is done to get you started.

There are 5 mice hidden in this picture
of the palace in the Kingdom of Sweets.
Find them and color them blue.

21

Fritz's toy soldiers all look alike, but only two
are identical. Find the matching pair
22 and color them red.

Help the candy-striped peppermint children
find their way back to Mother Ginger.

23

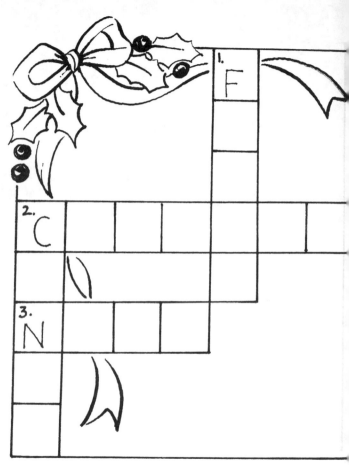

There are lots of goodies in the Kingdom of Sweets. Look at the pictures on the opposite page and fill in the crossword puzzle.

24

1. DOWN

2. ACROSS

2. DOWN

3. ACROSS

Clara's godfather Drosselmeyer has come to
visit, but 4 things seem very strange.
26   Find and circle them.

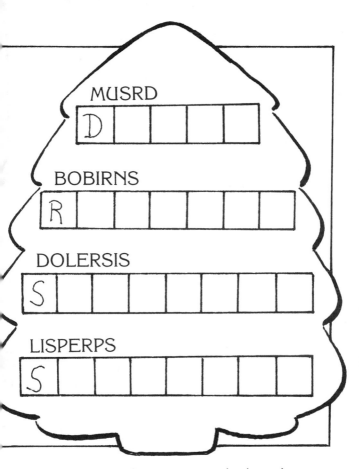

MUSRD

D

BOBIRNS

R

DOLERSIS

S

LISPERPS

S

Unscramble the letters to see what's under Clara's and Fritz's Christmas tree. The first letter of each word is in the right place.

27

CLARA

FRITZ

SOLDIER

MOUSE

The pictures above are from the story of the Nutcracker. Color them, then find their names in the puzzle on the opposite page.

Q	P	F	R	I	T	Z	O
E	O	N	I	S	L	I	M
T	S	R	M	O	U	S	E
C	A	C	E	L	T	N	L
L	B	J	O	D	Q	U	S
A	G	H	K	I	N	P	C
R	I	Z	U	E	A	Y	J
A	I	E	B	R	L	K	E

Words can go down and across.

29

1. ↓ It rhymes with sandy

2. → It rhymes
with pants

3. → It rhymes with boy

4. ↓ It rhymes with bee.

TREE

TOY

DANCE

CANDY

Use the clues and the words in the box to solve the puzzle. All of the answers rhyme.

Color this picture of Clara and the Prince in
the Kingdom of Sweets. 1=red; 2=green;
3=yellow; 4=brown; 5=blue.

Just 2 of the snowflake fairies are exactly
the same. Find the 2 that match
and color them blue.

33

Connect the dots to see what friendly animal pulled the sled that took Clara and the Prince home from the Kingdom of Sweets.

Draw the other half of the Nutcracker.
For help, copy the lines in each box
of the grid.

35

3. DOWN

2. ACROSS

4. ACROSS

1. DOWN

Use the picture clues to solve this
crossword puzzle.

Help the Sugarplum Fairy find her way
to her friend the Cavalier.

Two of the sugar-candy shepherdesses are
exactly alike. Can you find and circle them?

Here are 2 pictures of Clara and the Prince
traveling through the Enchanted Forest. Find

6 ways in which the pictures are different.

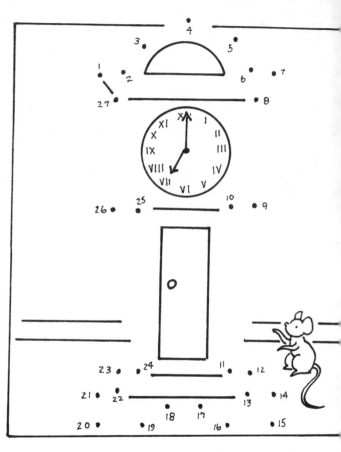

What's ticking in the Stahlbaum family's living room? Connect the dots to find out.

Follow the numbers to color this picture
of the Russian dancer who entertained Clara
and the Prince in the Kingdom of Sweets.
1=blue; 2=red; 3=black; 4=purple; 5=green. **43**

There are 7 birds hidden in the snowy
Enchanted Forest. Find them and color
them yellow.

The Nutcracker has lost his trusty sword.
Help him find his way through the maze
to get it back.

45

Look at the 2 pictures of Tea, the Chinese
Magician, and his 2 assistants. Can you find

the 6 ways in which they are different?

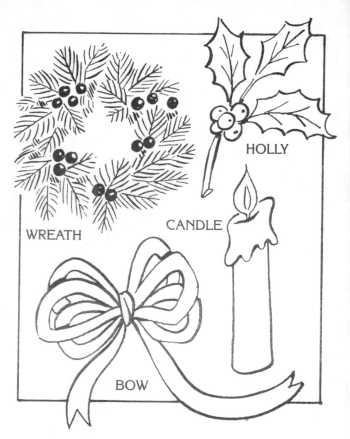

WREATH

HOLLY

CANDLE

BOW

Clara has decorated her house for Christmas.
Color these objects in holiday colors.
Then, find their names in the puzzle on the
opposite page. Words go across and down.

A	E	L	M	K	B	I	M
W	D	I	U	O	E	C	A
C	B	O	W	S	L	U	L
A	S	G	R	I	C	D	I
N	P	A	E	T	E	O	P
D	O	C	A	N	J	Z	R
L	R	Z	T	R	A	E	O
E	P	A	H	O	L	L	Y

CHRISTMAS

CART

How many words can you spell with
the letters in CHRISTMAS?

Clara is lost! Help her find the way back
to the Prince.

The Nutcracker is hidden in the pile of toys.
Find him and color him green.

Solutions

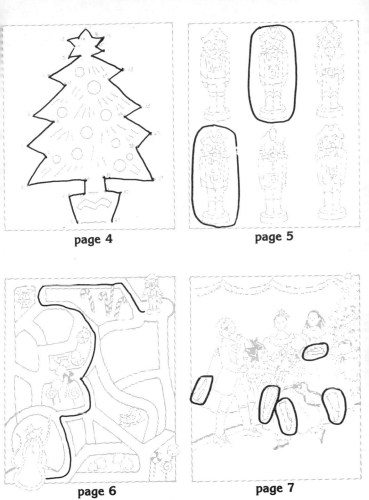

page 4

page 5

page 6

page 7

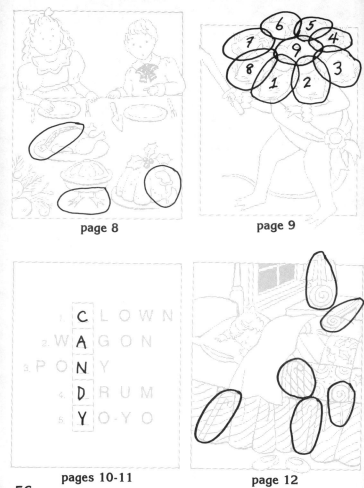

page 8

page 9

C L O W N
W A G O N
P O N Y
D R U M
Y O-Y O

pages 10-11

page 12

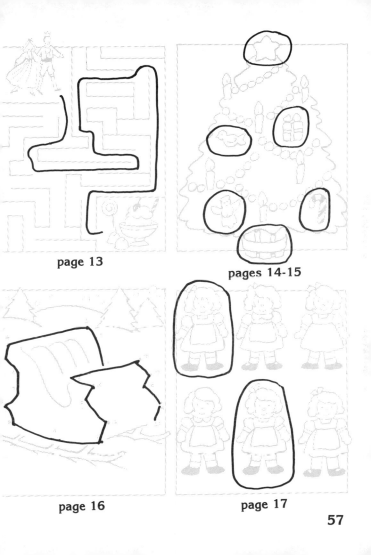

page 13

pages 14-15

page 16

page 17

How many soldiers do you count?
How many mice do you count?
How many are more all together?

6
14

pages 18-19

NUTCRACKER

CAKE	CAR
CANE	CART
RAKE	CARE
TAKE	TRACE

plus many more

page 20

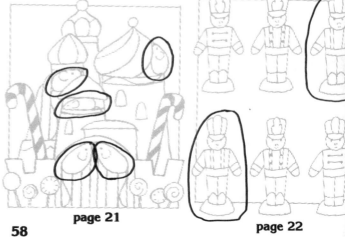

page 21

page 22

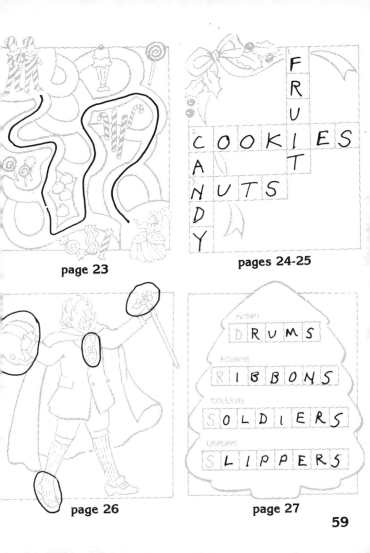

page 23

pages 24-25

page 26

page 27

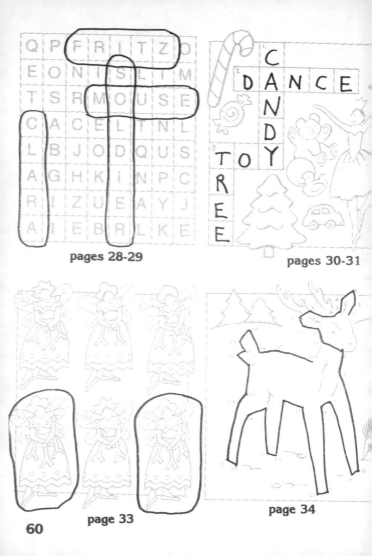

Q	P	F	R	I	T	Z	O
E	O	N	I	S	L	I	M
T	S	R	M	O	U	S	E
C	A	C	E	L	T	N	L
L	B	J	O	D	Q	U	S
A	G	H	K	I	N	P	C
R	I	Z	U	E	A	Y	J
A	I	E	B	R	L	K	E

pages 28-29

C
D A N C E
A
N
T O D Y
R
E
E

pages 30-31

60   **page 33**

page 34

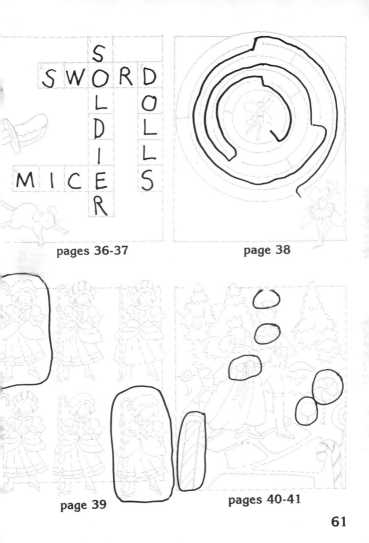

S
SWORD
O L
L I D
D O E
I L R
E L
MICE S
R

pages 36-37

page 38

page 39

pages 40-41

61

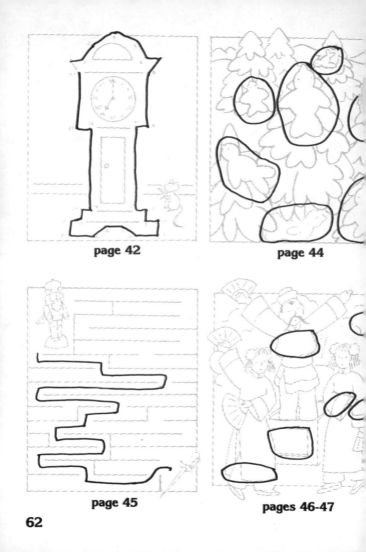

page 42

page 44

page 45

pages 46-47

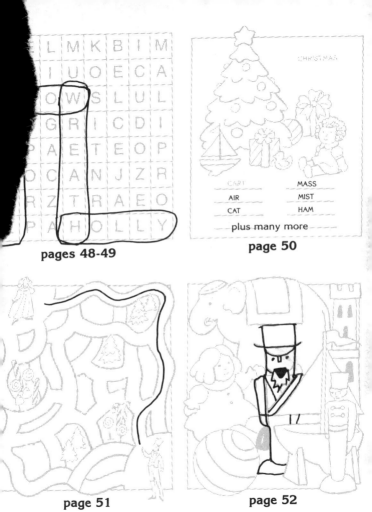

E	L	M	K	B	I	M
I	I	U	O	E	C	A
O	W	S	L	U	L
G	R	I	C	D	I
P	A	E	T	E	O	P
O	C	A	N	J	Z	R
R	Z	T	R	A	E	O
P	I	A	H	O	L	L	Y

pages 48-49

CHRISTMAS

CART	MASS
AIR	MIST
CAT	HAM

plus many more

page 50

page 51

page 52